Baby Blues® **13** Scrapbook

D1472091

I SHOULDN'T HAVE TO SCREAM MORE THAN ONCE !!!

Other Baby Blues® books from Andrews McMeel Publishing

Guess Who Didn't Take a Nap?
I Thought Labor Ended When the Baby Was Born
We Are Experiencing Parental Difficulties. . . Please Stand By
Night of the Living Dad
I Saw Elvis in My Ultrasound
One More and We're Outnumbered!
Check, Please. . .
threats, bribes & videotape
If I'm a Stay-At-Home Mom, Why Am I Always in the Car
Lift and Separate

Treasuries

The Super-Absorbent Biodegradable Family-Size Baby Blues®
Baby Blues®: Ten Years and Still in Diapers

Baby Blues® **13** Scrapbook

I SHOULDN'T HAVE TO SCREAM MORE THAN ONCE!!!

by
Rick Kirkman & Jerry Scott

**Andrews McMeel
Publishing**

Kansas City

Baby Blues is syndicated internationally by King Features Syndicate, Inc. For information, write King Features Syndicate, Inc., 235 East 45th Street, New York, New York 10017.

00 01 02 03 04 BAH 10 9 8 7 6 5 4 3 2

ISBN: 0-7407-0557-1

Library of Congress Catalog Card Number: 00-103477

Find *Baby Blues* on the Web at
www.babyblues.com

—— **ATTENTION: SCHOOLS AND BUSINESSES** ——

Andrews McMeel books are available at quantity discounts with bulk purchase for educational, business, or sales promotional use. For information, please write to: Special Sales Department, Andrews McMeel Publishing, 4520 Main Street, Kansas City, Missouri 64111.

For my Uncle Jerry and Aunt Elaine—thanks for the memories.
—R.K.

To all of our readers who have ever had a kid or been one . . . thank you.
—J.S.

The *Gourmet* Palate

The DISCERNING Palate

The PARENTAL Palate

8

11

SOMETHING YOU'D RATHER NOT BE WONDERING

APRIL

*Dear Tracey,
It's so exciting to hear that you're expecting.*

JULY

*Dear Tracey,
It's so exciting to hear that you're ~~expecting~~ being a new Mommy!*

DECEMBER

*Dear Tracey,
It's so exciting to hear that you're ~~expecting~~ being ~~a new Mommy!~~ thinking of going back to work!*

APRIL

*Dear Tracey,
It's so exciting to hear that you're ~~expecting being a new Mommy! thinking of going back to work;~~ expecting again!*

I'VE GOTTA CATCH UP ON MY CORRESPONDENCE!

I HAVEN'T SAID ANYTHING, BUT THIS PAST WEEK I THOUGHT THAT I MIGHT BE PREGNANT AGAIN.

BUT I'M NOT.

ISN'T THAT FUNNY?

"FUNNY" ISN'T THE WORD THAT FIRST LEAPS TO MIND.

WHAT ARE YOU DRINKING, DADDY?

COFFEE.

WHY? WHY? HOW?

BECAUSE I LIKE IT.

BECAUSE IT WAKES ME UP.

WELL, IT HAS CAFFEINE IN IT, AND CAFFEINE IS A THING THAT WAKES PEOPLE UP WHEN THEY'RE TIRED.

OH,

YEAH, EXCEPT COFFEE ISN'T AS LOUD AND IT DOESN'T NEED DIAPERS.

LIKE BABIES.

Panel 1: SO, HAMMIE IS GOING TO STAY WITH YOLANDA AND KEESHA TOMORROW WHILE I'M THE CLASSROOM VOLUNTEER IN YOUR PRESCHOOL CLASS!

Panel 2: YOU'RE GOING TO STAY THERE THE WHOLE MORNING?

YEP. THE WHOLE MORNING.

AND HELP THE TEACHER?

WHATEVER SHE NEEDS.

Panel 3:

Panel 4: PROMISE NOT TO EMBARRASS ME?

DON'T WORRY, I ALWAYS COLOR INSIDE THE LINES.

Panel 5: ZOE'S PRESCHOOL TEACHER ASKED ME TO BE THE CLASSROOM VOLUNTEER TOMORROW, AND I SAID YES.

REALLY? COOL.

Panel 6: WHAT DOES THE CLASSROOM VOLUNTEER DO?

Panel 7: OH, YOU KNOW... HANDS OUT SUPPLIES, PICKS UP CRAYONS, RUNS ERRANDS, CLEANS UP SPILLS, WIPES NOSES...

Panel 8: ...IN OTHER WORDS, EVERYTHING I DO AT HOME, BUT WITH FIFTEEN TIMES AS MANY KIDS.

ARE YOU SURE IT'S CALLED "CLASSROOM VOLUNTEER," AND NOT "CLASSROOM DRAFTEE"?

Panel 9: THANKS SO MUCH FOR BEING THE CLASSROOM VOLUNTEER TODAY, WANDA.

YOU'RE WELCOME!

Panel 10: NOW, DO YOU HAVE ANY QUESTIONS BEFORE WE GET STARTED?

JUST ONE...

Panel 11: ...ARE OTHER KIDS THIS CLINGY WHEN THEIR MOMS VOLUNTEER, OR IS IT JUST MINE?

ZOE, WOULD YOU LIKE TO INTRO-DUCE OUR HELPER TODAY?

THIS IS MY MOM. SHE'S THE CLASSROOM VOLUNTEER TODAY.

OTHER THAN THAT, I CAN'T THINK OF ANYTHING INTERESTING TO SAY ABOUT HER.

THANKS A LOT!

I'M TELLING YOU, BEING THE CLASSROOM VOLUNTEER IN ZOE'S ROOM GAVE ME A NEW APPRECIATION FOR HOW HARD TEACHERS WORK!

OH?

IT WAS **AMAZING**! THERE WAS STORY TIME, CRAFTS, PAINTING, PLAY TIME, SONG TIME...

EVERY MOMENT WAS CAREFULLY PLANNED OUT, EVERY ACTIVITY HAD A PURPOSE. WHAT AN ENRICHING EXPERIENCE!

WOW! SOUNDS GREAT!

HEY ZOE! TELL ME WHAT YOU DID IN SCHOOL TODAY.

NOTHIN'.

BBBBBBBBBBBB...

...BBBBBBBBBB...

HAMMIE, YOU'RE PUTTING TIRE TRACKS ALL OVER MOMMY'S KITCHEN CABINETS. TAKE YOUR TRUCK INTO THE LIVING ROOM TO PLAY, OKAY?

KKKXXXXT!

?

BEEP! BEEP! BEEP! BEEP!

BACK-UP SIGNAL.

SO WHAT ARE WE HAVING FOR DINNER TONIGHT, HONEY?

SOMETHING SIMPLE.

LIKE WHAT? POT ROAST?

THINK SIMPLER.

CHICKEN?

MEAT LOAF?

FISH?

THINK SIMPLER.

THINK SIMPLER.

THINK TAKE OUT.

! ! ! !

OH, ONE OF THOSE DAYS, HUH?

I AM PRINCESS HIGH 'N MIGHTY BIG SHOT TOLD-YOU-SO BOSS OF THE WORLD!

I KNOW EVERYTHING AND I GET WHATEVER I WANT WHENEVER I WANT IT!

EXCUSE ME WHILE I GO LOOK AT MYSELF IN THE MIRROR FOR A LONG TIME.

HEE! HEE! THE WORLD'S YOUNGEST TEENAGER!

YOU LAUGH NOW...

DINNER TIME!

WHAT ARE WE HAVING?

HAMBURGERS AND FRENCH FRIES!

OH.

WHAT'S WRONG? I THOUGHT YOU LIKED HAMBURGERS AND FRENCH FRIES.

I DO...

...THEY JUST DON'T TASTE AS GOOD WITHOUT A PLAYGROUND NEXT TO THEM.

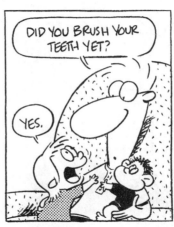

The REAL STICKER SHOCK

CAN WE GO EAT OUR LUNCH OVER BY THE SANDBOX?

WELL, YOU AND KEESHA CAN, BUT I'M GOING TO NURSE HAMMIE, SO HE HAS TO STAY WITH ME.

OH,

THAT'S THE TROUBLE WITH BEING A BABY... YOU CAN'T GET YOUR FOOD "TO-GO."

YEAH.

KIRKMAN & SCOTT

A, B, C, D, E, F, G...

...H, I, J, K, L, M, N, O, P...

...Q, R, S, T, U, V... UM...

WWW DOT X, Y, Z!

KIRKMAN & SCOTT

OKAY, THAT'S ENOUGH TV FOR A WHILE...

EEEEEEEK! CRASH! BANG! SCREEECH! KA-PINNGGG!

WHY DON'T YOU TWO GO PLAY A NICE GAME TOGETHER?

AHHH...

KIRKMAN & SCOTT

EEEEEEEK! CRASH! BANG! SCREEECH! KA-PINNGGG!

38

40

MOM, IS IT OKAY IF I LET BABYCAKES OUT OF HER CAGE FOR A WHILE?

WHY NOT?

MOM, IS IT OKAY IF I SIT ON THE COUCH AND HOLD BABYCAKES IN MY LAP?

WHY NOT?

MOM, IS IT OKAY IF BABYCAKES CRAWLS UNDER THE COUCH CUSHIONS AND WON'T COME OUT?

WHY ME?

KIRKMAN & SCOTT

WHAT DO YOU MEAN YOU LOST THE HAMSTER??

SOMETHING WRONG?

BABYCAKES CRAWLED DOWN BETWEEN THE COUCH CUSHIONS AND SHE WON'T COME OUT.

WE'LL SEE ABOUT THAT...

BE CAREFUL, DADDY!

DON'T WORRY... I WON'T HURT HER.

NO, I MEAN, BE CAREFUL BECAUSE SOMETIMES SHE BITES.

OWWW!

KIRKMAN & SCOTT

WE HAVE A HAMSTER CRAWLING AROUND INSIDE OUR COUCH! WHAT ARE WE GOING TO DO??

I DON'T THINK IT'S ANYTHING TO WORRY ABOUT.

THERE'S NOTHING DOWN THERE BUT LINT, COOKIE CRUMBS, PRETZEL PIECES AND POPCORN. BABYCAKES WILL PROBABLY GET BORED AND COME OUT...

KIRKMAN & SCOTT

CRUNCH! MUNCH! CHOMP! CHOMP! GULP!

...IN ABOUT A MONTH OR SO...

BOY, SHE SURE SOUNDS HAPPY!

BURP!

41

43

WOOO! WHAT A DAY!

ME, TOO!

MINE WAS NOTHING BUT PROBLEMS AND PRESSURE AND FRUSTRATION.

ME, TOO.

YOU'RE IN PRESCHOOL!

WE HAD TO COUNT TO TEN BY FIVES!

DADDY!

DADDY!

DADDY! I HAVE TO GO POTTY!

ALL DONE!

BUT YOU DIDN'T GO!

IT WAS JUST PRETEND POTTY.

THEN NEXT TIME PRETEND TO WAKE ME UP!

MOMMY! DADDY! HAMMIE IS PICKING UP OLD DIRTY PEAS OFF THE KITCHEN FLOOR AND PUTTING THEM IN HIS MOUTH!

¡GASP!

I FIGURE, AS LONG AS HE'S EATING, WE MIGHT AS WELL HIT ALL THE MAJOR FOOD GROUPS.

MOMMY! HAMMIE NEEDS A NEW DIAPER!

OH. OKAY.

WHY IS IT ALWAYS, "**MOMMY**, HAMMIE NEEDS A NEW DIAPER," AND NOT, "**DADDY**, HAMMIE NEEDS A NEW DIAPER"?

'CAUSE YOU DON'T PAY ME A QUARTER LIKE DADDY DOES.

UH-OH! TIME TO TAKE OUT THE TRASH...

47

WERE YOU KEEPING YOUR WRISTS STRAIGHT?

YES.

AND YOUR KNEES WERE BENT?

WERE YOUR FEET TOGETHER?

HMMMMM...

YES.

YES.

HONEY, COULD YOU COME OUT HERE FOR A SECOND?

KIRKMAN & SCOTT

ZOE NEEDS SOME JUMP ROPE LESSONS FROM YOU.

I THINK IT'S A GIRL THING.

WHAT ARE YOU WATCHING, DADDY?

THE BASKETBALL PRE-GAME SHOW.

WHAT'S THAT?

WELL, IT'S A SHOW WHERE A BUNCH OF PEOPLE TALK ABOUT WHAT'S GOING TO HAPPEN IN THE GAME, WHO WILL SCORE THE MOST POINTS AND WHAT KIND OF GAME IT WILL BE.

THEN THE PLAYERS PLAY THE GAME.

THEN WHAT?

KIRKMAN & SCOTT

WHY?

51

GASP! YOU BROKE MY VASE!

GRANDMA WIZOWSKI GAVE ME THAT VASE!

I'VE ALWAYS SORT OF HATED THAT VASE...

BUT YOU'RE **STILL** IN TROUBLE!

AUGGGGHH! YOU'RE DRIVING ME **NUTS**!! WILL YOU PLEASE KNOCK IT OFF?

BONG! BONG! BONG! BONG! BONG! BONG!

WHAT DO I GET IF I DO?

CAVITIES FOR SANITY... SEEMS LIKE A FAIR TRADE.

WHERE DID YOU GET BUBBLEGUM?

KIRKMAN & SCOTT

DOGGIE!

NO, ZOE!

YOU SHOULD **NEVER** RUN UP TO A STRANGE DOG.

WHY?

SOME DOGS GET SCARED AROUND PEOPLE THEY DON'T KNOW, SO YOU SHOULD ALWAYS ASK THE OWNER IF IT'S SAFE TO PET THEIR DOG FIRST.

OH.

IS YOUR DOGGIE FRIENDLY?

HE LIKES KIDS.

NICE BOY!...

GRRRR!

KIRKMAN & SCOTT

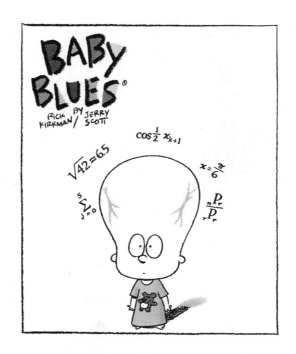

Panel 1: MOMMY! DADDY! HAMMIE JUST WENT POTTY ALL BY HIMSELF! / HE DID? / ARE YOU KIDDING?

Panel 2: THIS IS UNBELIEVABLE! / IT'S FANTASTIC! AND HE'S ONLY FOURTEEN MONTHS OLD!

Panel 3: AREN'T YOU GOING TO ASK ME **WHERE** HE WENT?

KIRKMAN & SCOTT

Panel 4: I AM PRINCESS HIGH N' MIGHTY BIG-SHOT TOLD-YOU-SO BOSS OF THE WORLD, AND **THIS** IS PRINCE BOBO. / HI.

Panel 5: YOU MUST DO WHATEVER I COMMAND BECAUSE **I AM THE PRINCESS.** / YEAH!

Panel 6: IF I WANT ICE CREAM, YOU MUST GIVE ME ICE CREAM! IF I WANT CANDY, YOU MUST GIVE ME CANDY! IS THAT CLEAR? / YAY!

Panel 7: YOU AND YOUR BIG MOUTH.

KIRKMAN & SCOTT

Panel 8: I DON'T KNOW HOW YOU DO IT, WANDA.

Panel 9: YOU'RE A STAY-AT-HOME MOM WITH TWO KIDS, A CLASSROOM VOLUNTEER AT ZOE'S PRESCHOOL, AND YOU **STILL** FIND TIME TO BE ENVIRONMENTALLY RESPONSIBLE.

Panel 10: YOU'RE **AMAZING!**

Panel 11: THIS ISN'T A RECYCLING PILE... IT'S THE NEWSPAPERS AND MAGAZINES I HAVEN'T HAD A CHANCE TO READ THIS MONTH!

KIRKMAN & SCOTT

BABY BLUES®

BY RICK KIRKMAN / JERRY SCOTT

WHAT'S GOING ON?

HAMMIE HAS A RASH.

ALLERGIES?

MAYBE. I'VE NEVER SEEN ANYTHING LIKE THIS.

HE'S NEVER BEEN ALLERGIC TO ANYTHING BEFORE, HAS HE?

NO, BUT KIDS CAN DEVELOP ALLERGIES AT ANYTIME.

THE TRICK IS TO FIGURE OUT WHAT COULD HAVE CAUSED IT. PROBABLY SOMETHING HE WAS EXPOSED TO TODAY...

STRAWBERRIES? CITRUS? WHEAT?

SIBLING.

DOT...DOT... DOT...DOT... DOT...

63

BABY BLUES®

BY RICK KIRKMAN / JERRY SCOTT

SO WHAT'S GOING ON TODAY?

NOT MUCH.

ZOE IS GOING TO PLAY AT KEESHA'S HOUSE FROM 8:30 TO 9:45 WHILE HAMMIE AND I GO TO HIS DOCTOR APPOINTMENT. THEN WE'LL SWING BY THE GROCERY STORE AND THE DRY CLEANER ON THE WAY HOME. I'LL PUT THE GROCERIES AWAY, THEN PICK UP ZOE, KEESHA AND BOGART AND TAKE EVERYBODY OVER TO THE PARK FOR HALF AN HOUR. BUNNY AND YOLANDA WILL MEET US THERE AT 10:15, AND WE'LL ALL GO TO THE PUPPET SHOW FROM 10:30 TO 11:00. THEN LUNCH, HOME FOR NAP TIME, UP TO THE COMMUNITY CENTER AT 2:00 FOR SWIMMING LESSONS, A FEW MORE ERRANDS, AND THEN HOME AGAIN TO MAKE DINNER.

"NOT MUCH" MEANS A **TOTALLY DIFFERENT** THING TO MOTHERS THAN IT DOES TO FATHERS.

LOOK, ZOE. YOU NEED TO STOP QUESTIONING ME EVERY TIME I TELL YOU TO DO SOMETHING.

I'M YOUR MOTHER. I GAVE BIRTH TO YOU, AND I KNOW WHAT'S BEST FOR YOU.

I DIDN'T GET THIS JOB BECAUSE OF MY GOOD LOOKS.

WELL, ACTUALLY...

I'M NOT TALKING TO YOU.

HI, MOMMY, DO YOU WANT TO BE IN MY SECRET CLUB?

SECRET CLUB? I DON'T KNOW... WHAT DO YOU DO?

WELL, I'M IN CHARGE OF IDEAS AND GAMES, AND HAMMIE IS IN CHARGE OF CARRYING STUFF.

AND WHAT WOULD I BE IN CHARGE OF?

MAKING SNACKS AND CLEANING UP.

THAT'S NOT A SECRET CLUB... THAT'S MY LIFE.

EXCEPT YOU GET TO WEAR A HAT!

ZOE! HAMMIE! I HEAR WHAT'S GOING ON IN THERE! KNOCK IT OFF!

OKAY, MOMMY, SORRY.

WOW! GOOD EARS.

I DIDN'T REALLY HEAR ANYTHING... I JUST WENT WITH THE ODDS.

KIRKMAN & SCOTT

67

68

69

WOULD YOU GET THE KIDS READY FOR BED TONIGHT BY YOURSELF? I'M WHIPPED.

SURE, HONEY, NO PROBLEM. YOU TAKE IT EASY, AND I'LL HANDLE EVERYTHING. DON'T WORRY ABOUT A THING.

SO, WHAT DO I DO FIRST?

WOW! **THAT'S** A GREAT NIGHTIE!

YOU LOOK SENSATIONAL! JUST BEAUTIFUL! REALLY, REALLY BEAUTIFUL!

THANK YOU.

THE KIDS WON'T RECOGNIZE YOU.

WORN-OUT CARPETING... DENTED BASEBOARDS... SCRATCHED-UP FURNITURE... STICKY DOORKNOBS...

HALF THE THINGS IN THIS HOUSE NEED TO BE FIXED OR CLEANED...

...AND THE OTHER HALF ARE STILL OUT OF REACH.

NO GOOD. WE NEED A LONGER STICK.

KIRKMAN & SCOTT

ATTENTION, PLEASE!! I HAVE AN ANNOUNCEMENT!!

ANNOUNCEMENT! ANNOUNCEMENT! VERY IMPORTANT ANNOUNCEMENT COMING UP!!

OKAY, WHAT'S THE BIG ANNOUNCEMENT?

I FOUND MY OLD MEGAPHONE!!

WHAT SHOULD WE READ TONIGHT, ZOE... "IF YOU GIVE A MOUSE A COOKIE," OR "GO DOG GO"?

I WANT THIS.

ARCHITECTURAL DIGEST AGAIN??

GO WITH IT, DARRYL! IF ZOE LIKES ARCHITECTURE, IT MAKES SENSE TO READ TO HER ABOUT ARCHITECTURE!

YEAH!

BESIDES, IT PUTS HIM TO SLEEP FASTER.

MOM, CAN WE HAVE SOME COOKIES?

NO, NO, NO NO NO!

COOKIES!

HOW MANY TIMES DO I HAVE TO SAY, "NO MORE COOKIES"??

IF WE GUESS RIGHT, DO WE GET SOME COOKIES?

72

LET'S GO! LET'S GO, GUPPIES!

SOMETHING WRONG, JAKE?

I GOT A BOO-BOO.

KISS! THERE YOU GO. IS THAT BETTER?

SNIF! YEAH.

LOOK ALIVE OUT THERE GANG! WE HAVE TO BE—

WHAT DO YOU NEED, ZOE?

I'M SCARED OF THE BALL AGAIN.

AWWW...THERE'S NO REASON TO BE AFRAID OF THE BALL, SWEETHEART...JUST DO WHAT YOU DID IN PRACTICE YESTERDAY!

OKAY, DADDY.

COACH! STANLEY CALLED ME A POOPHEAD!

WELL, MADDIE, I'M SURE HE DIDN'T MEAN IT, BUT I'LL HAVE A TALK WITH HIM ANYWAY.

LET'S GO GUPPIES! LET'S SEE A LITTLE—

—UH...

THIS ISN'T T-BALL...IT'S GROUP THERAPY WITH UNIFORMS.

THE SHORTSTOP STUCK HER TONGUE OUT AT ME!

BEN IS ASLEEP IN THE OUTFIELD AGAIN!

TELL HIM TO STOP MAKING KISSING NOISES AT ME!

T-BALL MAKE MY DOZE RUN!

I NEED A HUG!

SECOND BASE IS TOO SCARY!

SMOOOOCH! SMOOOCH!

CHARLIE HORSE! CHARLIE HORSE!

MY MOM SAYS I'M TOO CUTE TO BE THE CATCHER!

DINING WITHOUT THE KIDS

DINING WITH THE KIDS

77

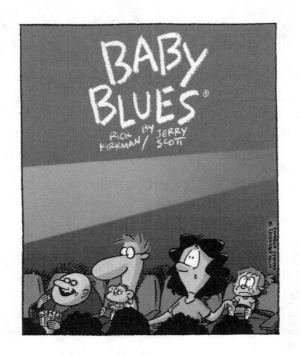

WOW! I LOVED THAT MOVIE!! IT WAS SCARY AND FUNNY AND I DIDN'T EVEN GET BORED ONCE!

CLAP! CLAP! CLAP!

CLAP! CLAP! CLAP!

LET'S GO HAVE ICE CREAM!

ZOE! GET BACK HERE! THOSE WERE JUST THE PREVIEWS!

HEY, ZOE! COME TELL ME ABOUT YOUR DAY!

SO, DID YOU PLAY?

DID YOU DRAW?

DID YOU GO SWIMMING?

I DON'T KNOW.

I DON'T KNOW.

I DON'T KNOW.

OKAY, THEN LET ME TELL YOU ABOUT MY DAY...

I BET IT WASN'T AS MUCH FUN AS MINE!

OOOH! MY BACK IS KILLING ME!

AGAIN?? DO YOU THINK IT COULD BE THE BED?

MAYBE, BUT OUR MATTRESS IS ONLY TWO YEARS OLD...

...I DON'T KNOW HOW SOMETHING THAT EXPENSIVE COULD FALL APART SO QUICKLY.

ONE, TWO! BUCKLE MY SHOE!

THREE, FOUR! BUCKLE MY SHOE!

FIVE, SIX! BUCKLE MY SHOE!

SEVEN, EIGHT! BUCKLE MY SHOE!

THAT'S VERY GOOD, ZOE, BUT YOUR POEM DOESN'T MAKE ANY SENSE.

I KNOW... ALL MY SHOES FASTEN WITH VELCRO.

KIRKMAN & SCOTT

WHAT ARE YOU DOING IN HERE?

I DIDN'T WANT TO SLEEP BY MYSELF.

WELL, THERE ISN'T ENOUGH ROOM FOR ALL OF US IN HERE, SO...

...SO...

THANKS, DADDY!

DARN "BAMBI" EYES!

NOW, IF YOU WAKE UP IN THE MIDDLE OF THE NIGHT, YOU'RE GOING TO STAY IN BED, RIGHT?

RIGHT.

SO WHAT HAPPENS IF YOU WAKE UP IN THE MIDDLE OF THE NIGHT?

I STAY IN BED.

GOOD, SEE YOU IN THE MORNING.

12:01 AM

HI.

DADDY IS GOING TO SIT HERE UNTIL YOU FALL ASLEEP. THAT WAY YOU'LL FEEL SAFE AND YOU WON'T HAVE TO COME INTO OUR BED AGAIN TONIGHT.

OKAY.

DID YOU KNOW DADDY SNORES WHEN HE SLEEPS SITTING UP?

82

83

BABY BLUES®

BY RICK KIRKMAN / JERRY SCOTT

NO NO NO NO NO NO

NO!

OH, GREAT. HAMMIE IS STARTING THE "NO" PHASE.

NO! NO!

WHAT'S THAT?

THE "NO" PHASE IS WHEN BABIES START WANTING TO MAKE THEIR OWN DECISIONS, AND THEY SHOW IT BY SAYING "NO" TO ALMOST EVERYTHING.

NO! NO! NO! NO!

WHY?

WELL, DISAGREEING IS THE EASIEST WAY FOR A PERSON TO GET ATTENTION AND TO SHOW THAT HE HAS A MIND OF HIS OWN.

NO! NO! NO! NO! NO! NO! NO! NO!

YOU KNOW, IF YOU LET HAMMIE PICK THE GAMES YOU PLAY AND EVEN LET HIM GO FIRST SOMETIMES, I'LL BET HE WOULD GET THROUGH THE "NO" PHASE SOONER!

NO! NO! NO! NO! NO! NO! NO! NO! NO!

YES! YES! YES! YES! YES! YES! YES!

ANY MORE BRILLIANT PSYCHOLOGICAL ADVICE, DR. SPOCK?

TONIGHT I WANT YOU TWO TO TAKE YOUR BATHS, BRUSH YOUR TEETH AND GO TO BED WITHOUT **ANY** WHINING OR COMPLAINING, UNDERSTAND?

BUT...

YES, MOM! WHATEVER YOU SAY!

OKIE-DOKIE!

HOW DID YOU—?

NEVER UNDERESTIMATE THE POWER OF A BRAND-NEW BOX OF FUDGESICLES.

NO BANGING ON YOUR DRUM, NO YELLING, NO RUNNING AROUND, AND NO MAKING NOISE, OKAY, HAMMIE??

OKAY!!

HOW COME?

HOW COME?

HEADACHE.

'CUZ MOMMY HAS A HEADACHE!!

WHAT??

HI, DADDY. I WAS JUST CALLING TO SAY I LOVE YOU.

HI, SWEETHEART. HOW NICE!

IS THAT ALL?

YES.

ARE YOU SURE?

UMMMM...

LOOK, ZOE, I'VE BEEN A DADDY FOR OVER FIVE YEARS...

OKAY! OKAY! AND I ALSO ACCIDENTALLY POURED A LITTLE MAPLE SYRUP IN THE VCR.

HEY, ZOE! WANT TO PLAY CATCH WITH ME?

NO.

WANT TO GO FOR A WALK?

READ A BOOK TOGETHER?

RIDE OUR BIKES?

NO.

NO.

NO.

WELL, OKAY...

DADDY'S IGNORING ME!!

I READ AN ARTICLE SOMEWHERE THAT LISTENING TO MOZART CAN ACTUALLY MAKE KIDS SMARTER.

YEAH, RIGHT.

THEY SAID THAT THE VERY PRECISE MATHEMATICAL PATTERNS OF HIS MUSIC SORT OF RESHUFFLE THE BRAIN'S SYNAPSES AND STIMULATE MORE ORGANIZED THOUGHT PATTERNS.

SURE... SURE...

WHEEE! BANG! BANG! POW! SCREEEEECH! I GOT YOU! DID NOT!

PLUS, IT ALSO CALMS THEM DOWN.

BRING IT ON, WOLFGANG!

THACK!

!#@%*!!

PROFANITY AND ROCK'N'ROLL ARE THE TWO THINGS THAT ARE MOST SATISFYING AT FULL VOLUME.

THAT'S ODD.

WHAT IS?

IT'S SEVEN-THIRTY ON A SATURDAY MORNING AND THE HOUSE IS STILL QUIET.

NO NOISY KIDS... NO MINDLESS CARTOONS BLARING ON THE TV...

WELL, I GUESS I'D BETTER SAVOR IT WHILE I CAN!

SAVOR IT QUICKLY.

BABY BLUES®

BY RICK KIRKMAN / JERRY SCOTT

DID YOU HEAR WHAT THE AMERICAN ACADEMY OF PEDIATRICS SAID ABOUT KIDS AND TELEVISION?

NO, WHAT?

THEY SAY THAT KIDS UNDER THE AGE OF TWO SHOULDN'T WATCH TV AT ALL.

WHY NOT?

WELL, THEY SAY TODDLERS NEED DIRECT INTERACTION WITH REAL PEOPLE FOR HEALTHY BRAIN GROWTH AND DEVELOPMENT OF SOCIAL, EMOTIONAL AND COGNITIVE SKILLS.

WELL, SURE... BUT NO TV AT ALL? NOT EVEN A LITTLE SESAME STREET, OR AN OCCASIONAL BARNEY VIDEO WHILE I FIX DINNER?

NONE.

NOPE. THEY CALL THAT "ELECTRONIC BABY-SITTING."

BEEP! BEEP! BEEP!

GOOD MORNING... AMERICAN ACADEMY OF PEDIATRICS.

PPBBBBBTHHH!

KIRKMAN & SCOTT

SO, IF THE BIG HAND IS ON TWELVE, AND THE LITTLE HAND IS ON THE SEVEN, WHAT TIME IS IT?

UM...

...SEVEN O'CLOCK...

...SIX CENTRAL, FIVE PACIFIC. ONLY ON THESE STATIONS.

I THOUGHT WE WERE CUTTING DOWN ON TV THIS SUMMER!!

OOOOH! MALE RAGE! WE SAW THIS ON OPRAH!

KIRKMAN & SCOTT

...AND MOM BOUGHT ME THESE NEW JEANS, AN' THIS NEW SHIRT, AN' THOSE NEW SWEATERS, AN' THESE NEW SHOES AN' EVEN THESE NEW SOCKS!

DON'T YOU JUST **LOVE** THIS STUFF?

YEAH, ZOE! YOU'RE REALLY GOING TO LOOK SPIFFY ON YOUR FIRST DAY OF KINDERGARTEN!

KINDERGARTEN?

YEAH, YOU START NEXT WEEK.

I **KNEW** THERE WAS A CATCH!!

THANKS FOR HELPING ME EASE HER INTO THE IDEA.

KIRKMAN & SCOTT

WHY DO I HAVE TO GO TO KINDERGARTEN??

ZOE, KINDERGARTEN IS GOING TO BE FUN!

YEAH! KINDERGARTEN IS GREAT! YOU'LL HAVE A GREAT TIME... MAKE NEW FRIENDS... LEARN NEW STUFF...

YOU'RE GOING TO LOVE IT. I PROMISE.

GUARANTEED OR MY MONEY BACK?

THIS IS SCHOOL WE'RE TALKING ABOUT HERE... NOT A MAJOR APPLIANCE.

PUBLIC EDUCATION DOESN'T COME WITH A WARRANTY, SWEETHEART.

KIRKMAN & SCOTT

BUT WHY DO I HAVE TO GO TO KINDERGARTEN?

I TOLD YOU! SO YOU CAN **LEARN** STUFF!

YOU'LL PRACTICE THE ALPHABET...

I ALREADY **KNOW** THE ALPHABET.

...STUDY NUMBERS...

I CAN ALREADY COUNT TO A HUNDRED.

...PRACTICE WRITING YOUR NAME...

I ALREADY KNOW HOW TO WRITE MY NAME, YOUR NAME, DADDY'S NAME AND HAMMIE'S NAME, TOO.

THEY SERVE COOKIES AND JUICE EVERY DAY AT 10:30.

WHAT KIND?

I THINK THAT'S EVERYTHING.

WE HAVE HER LUNCH...

...HER SNACK...

...A BOTTLE OF WATER...

...EXTRA SNEAKERS, A SWEATER, A JACKET AND HER SCHOOL SUPPLIES.

CHECK.

CHECK.

CHECK.

CHECK, CHECK AND CHECK.

CAN YOU THINK OF ANYTHING ELSE ZOE MIGHT NEED FOR HER FIRST DAY OF KINDERGARTEN?

BESIDES A SHERPA?

WHAT KINDERGARTNERS LOOK LIKE ON THE FIRST DAY OF SCHOOL...

KIRKMAN & SCOTT

SNAP FLASH! BZZZZT! POP!

WHY...

FLASH! PHWEEEET! BZZT!

LOOK AT THIS!

WHAT IS IT?

I FILLED UP THIS ENTIRE GARBAGE BAG WITH TEENY LITTLE DOLL PARTS, ACCESSORIES, LOST GAME PIECES AND BROKEN TOYS FROM ZOE'S ROOM.

THERE WAS STUFF EVERYWHERE! IN HER CLOSET... UNDER HER BED... BEHIND THE DRESSER... UNDER THE RUG...

I'LL BET THERE ARE THOUSANDS OF PIECES OF JUNK IN THAT BAG THAT SHE FORGOT SHE EVEN—

GOOD! EVERYTHING SEEMS TO BE HERE!

—OWNED.

IT'S OKAY IF YOU PLAY WITH MY STUFF, MOMMY, BUT JUST BE SURE TO PUT EVERYTHING BACK WHERE YOU FOUND IT.

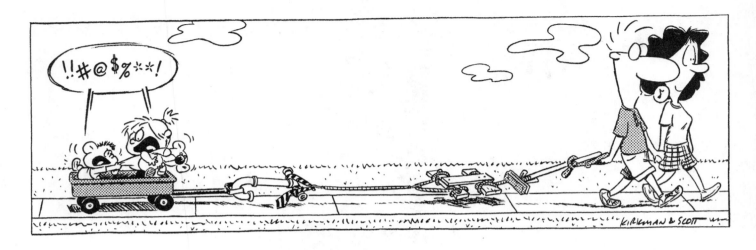

111

:SNORT!: MOMMY, CAN WE HAVE A SNACK? :GIGGLE!:

AAAARGH!

LOOK, ZOE...WE'VE PLAYED GAMES, BAKED COOKIES, MADE POPCORN, WATCHED MOVIES AND READ STORIES. WHAT IS IT GOING TO TAKE TO GET YOU GIRLS TO STOP GIGGLING AND GO TO SLEEP?

I NEED YOUR WALLET.

THEY'RE FINALLY ASLEEP.

HOW'D YOU DO IT?

WELL, I FIGURED THAT THE ONLY WAY TO MAKE THEM SLEEPY WAS TO SIT DOWN AND TELL THEM THE LONGEST, MOST DRAWN-OUT, EXHAUSTING STORY I COULD THINK OF.

WHICH WAS...?

I DESCRIBED MY DAY.

AH!

BYE, KEESHA! THANKS FOR SPENDING THE NIGHT!

IT WAS FUN!

SAY, "THANK YOU."

BYE-BYE! THANK YOU!

:CLICK!:

ZZZZZZZ

I DO-O-O-N'T WANNNA GO TO-O-O KINDERGA-A-A-ARTEN TODA-A-A-AY!

HOMEWORK. Have your child take twenty miniature marshmallows in one hand.

Now divide the marshmallows into groups of two. How many groups are there?

OKAY GUYS...DO YOU REMEMBER YOUR LINE?

TWICKER TWEET!

HAR! HAR! HE CAN'T EVEN SAY, "TRICK OR TREAT"! WHAT A BABY!

KNOCK IT OFF, ZOE. HE'S DOING FINE.

WELL, HE IS A BABY! HE SHOULDN'T EVEN BE OUT HERE IF HE CAN'T SAY THE WORDS RIGHT!

DING DONG!

TWICKER TWEET!

OH! AREN'T YOU ADORABLE!!

SHAKE! SHAKE! SHAKE!

HOW DID THAT GO AGAIN?

117

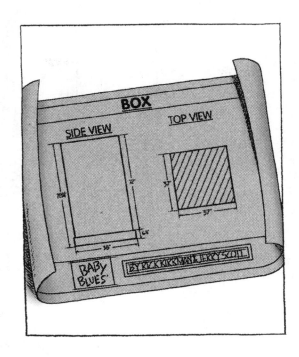

120

WANDA, WHAT WAS IT THAT MADE YOU DECIDE TO STAY HOME WITH THE KIDS INSTEAD OF GOING BACK TO WORK?

SEVERAL THINGS, I GUESS.

THE CONTINUITY, THE PEACE OF MIND, THE CHALLENGE...

LUNCH!

...NOT TO MENTION THE GLAMOR.

CHOMP! CHOMP! GULP! GULP!

WHAT DID THE KIDS DO TODAY?

KIDS! KIDS! KIDS! IT'S ALWAYS ABOUT THE KIDS!

WHY DOES EVERYTHING WE EVER TALK ABOUT HAVE TO REVOLVE AROUND THE KIDS??

OKAY! I'M **SORRY**! YOU'RE RIGHT!

WHAT DID **YOU** DO TODAY?

WATCHED THE KIDS.

WHAT ARE YOU LOOKING FOR, ZOE?

STUFF TO PLAY WITH.

WHAT KIND OF "STUFF"?

CARTOON STUFF. YOU KNOW... A ROCKET, A BIG MALLET, A STEAMROLLER, AN ANVIL....

GET YOUR SHOES... MOM'S TAKING US TO THE LIBRARY AGAIN.

CLICK!

WHATCHA' WORKING ON, ZOE?

HOMEWORK.

IS IT HARD?

DAD, I'M FIVE YEARS OLD. I'M IN KINDERGARTEN. I'M WORKING WITH CRAYONS...

OF **COURSE** IT'S HARD!!

JUST ASKING....

KIRKMAN & SCOTT

CAN I HAVE THREE CHOCOLATE CHIPS, PLEASE?

SURE.

MMMMMMMMMM...

AND HERE ARE THREE FOR HAMMIE.

YOU SURE KNOW HOW TO RUIN A GOOD THING.

MMMMMM...

KIRKMAN & SCOTT

HI, ZOE! HOW WAS SCHOOL TODAY?

GOOD.

DID YOU HAVE FUN?

YES.

DID ANYTHING EXCITING HAPPEN?

I GOT MARRIED TO MATTHEW GIOSEFFI AT RECESS.

SCREECH!

KIRKMAN & SCOTT

Panel 1: HERE'S YOUR HAMBURGER CASSEROLE. / WHAT'S HAMBURGER MADE OUT OF?

Panel 2: BEEF. / OH. OKAY.

Panel 3: AS LONG AS IT'S NOT COW. I LOVE COWS.

Panel 4: UH, ZOE, I TOLD YOU THAT THIS HAMBURGER IS MADE OUT OF BEEF... BUT WHAT I DIDN'T EXPLAIN IS THAT BEEF IS MADE OUT OF COWS. / IT IS??

Panel 5: THEN WHAT'S **HAM** MADE OUT OF? / PIGS.

Panel 6: POOR COWS! POOR PIGS! / NEXT THING I KNOW, YOU'RE GOING TO TELL ME THAT CHICKEN IS MADE OUT OF —

Panel 7: GASP!

Panel 8: WHY DOES MEAT HAVE TO BE MADE OUT OF ANIMALS? / WELL, ZOE, THAT'S JUST THE WAY IT IS!

Panel 9: BUT I **LOVE** ANIMALS! THEY'RE SO **CUTE!** / YES, BUT...

Panel 10: WHY CAN'T WE EAT STUFF MADE OUT OF THINGS THAT AREN'T **CUTE?** / LIKE WHAT?

Panel 11: LIKE SNAILS, OR CENTIPEDES, OR LITTLE BROTHERS, OR... / I THINK I'LL JUST HAVE THE CARROT SALAD TONIGHT.